Gaia a

Green Ethics

Implications of Ecological Theology

by
Celia Deane-Drummond

Consultant to ICOREC, Manchester
Visiting Lecturer in Theology for Extra-Mural Department, Manchester University

'God's Grandeur'
The world is charged with the grandeur of God.
It will flame out, like shining from snook foil,
It gathers to a greatness, like the ooze of oil.
Crushed, Why do men then now not reck his rod?
Generations have trod, have trod, have trod;
And all is seared with trade; bleared, smeared with toil;
And wears man's smudge and share's man's smell: the soil
Is bare now nor can foot feel, being shod.

And for all this, nature is never spent;
There lives the dearest freshness deep down things;
And though the last lights off the black West went
Oh, morning, at the brown brink eastward, springs.
because the Holy Ghost over thee went
World broods with warm breast and with ah! bright wings.
Gerard Manley Hopkins

GROVE BOOKS LIMITED
Bramcote   Nottingham   NG9 3DS

CONTENTS

THE COVER PICTURE

is by Greg Forster

ACKNOWLEDGEMENTS

I am very grateful to the following colleagues who commented on the original draft of the text and made many helpful suggestions: Canon Colin Bradley, Rev. Keith Innes and Rev. John Butterfield.

First Impression January 1993

ISSN 0951-2667

ISBN 1 85174 230 1

1. INTRODUCTION

The above poem is an example of the way the poetic imagination has kept alive a deep sense of the unity of all things as well as the horror of human-kind's destruction of the environment. As facts about the scale, size and urgency of ecological problems continue to accumulate we can react negatively in a number of ways. Either we feel, as individuals, powerless to do anything and suffer silently in solidarity with creation. Or, we become hardened in our thinking and no longer respond to these issues, anaesthetized by an overdose of information.[1] The purpose of this booklet is to rediscover positive ways of bringing our Christian faith to bear on these issues. This task is both in terms of:

(a) Broader concerns about the ethos or cultural milieu in which we find ourselves.

(b) Specific ethical problems such as the preservation of species.

The *Gaia* hypothesis fits into category (a) by encouraging us to perceive the world in a way that is different from that normally classified as science.[2] This hypothesis raises a number of fascinating questions about the way we value ourselves and the natural world. For example, one view of scientific theory is that the truth of the latter is tested by its power to control the world. In this sense the *Gaia* hypothesis is ambivalent: are we empowered or rendered powerless by it? In order to discover some of the reasons why *Gaia* has become a popular 'myth' we will trace some of the historical factors which led to the ecological crisis.[3]

(1) Historical Background to the Ecological Crisis
It is possible that Greek philosophy contributed to the prevention of the development of an ecological perspective. According to one American

---

[1] For a summary of the current extent of the ecological crisis see K. Innes: *Caring for the Earth* (Grove Ethical Studies no 66, Second Edition, 1991) pp.3-5. See references p.1, and also, *Caring for the Earth: A Strategy for Sustainable Living*, (IUCN/UNEP/WEWF, Gland, Switzerland, 1991).

[2] The *Gaia* hypothesis as defined formally by James Lovelock states that: 'The temperature, oxidation state, acidity, and certain aspects of rocks and waters are at any time kept constant, and that this homneostrasis is maintained by active feedback processes operated automatically and unconsciously by the biota.' (J. Lovelock, *Gaia* (Oxford University Press, Second Edition, 1987) p.19). The controversial aspect with respect to science is that the earth as a whole is 'alive', which Lovelock admits is 'at the outer bounds of scientific credibility', (p.3). There are other problems with the *Gaia* hypothesis from the scientific perspective, for a discussion see, C. Deane-Drummond, 'God and *Gaia*: Myth or Reality?' in *Theology* (July, 1992) pp.275-283; L. Osborn, 'The Machine and the Mother Goddess: The *Gaia* Hypothesis in Contemporary Scientific and Religious Thought', in *Science and Christian Belief*, 4 (1992) pp.27-41. For a further description of the *Gaia* hypothesis see section 2.

[3] A full treatment of the historical factors involved is outside the scope of this booklet. A lively debate about the historical interpretation of the biblical concept of dominion from Genesis 1.28 was begun when Lyn White, the medieval historian who is a specialist in medieval technology, blamed Christianity for encouraging an exploitative attitude to nature. His article has been criticized as an exaggerated account of the history of interpretation of Genesis 1.28. Other strands in the Christian tradition point towards an ecological responsibility. See K. Innes, *op. cit.*, p.14; L. White, 'The Historical Roots of our Ecologic Crisis' in *Science*, 155 (1967) pp.418-420.

3

philosopher the Greeks ignored complex relationships in search of rational structures, and admired order and beauty rather than the world as it is.[1] In other words a dominant strand in the Greek understanding of knowledge is that which is directed towards permanent, unchanging and eternal objects. This contrasts with the world of ecological relationships which are impermanent, perishable and in a constant state of flux. His view is oversimplified in that he does not allow for the irrational side of Greek thought and the concept of intuition in Plato which influenced poets such as Shelley and Hopkins. Also, as Robin Attfield, the British philosopher of environmental ethics, points out, Greek and Roman Christians were grounded in the reality of the created world and were aware of its mortality.[2] Nonetheless, the ultimately dominant side of Greek philosophy stressed impassible absolutes which may have paved the way for a subsequent development of a harsh attitude towards the natural world.

The influence of Descartes in shaping an anti-environmental bias is less controversial. He distrusted sensation and relied on reason to gain knowledge. While there was a strong empiricist tradition in the seventeenth century, modern explanations of science in terms of mathematics has tended to undercut the legitimacy of the environmental and natural history sciences. The triumph of fact over value culminated in the *logical positivists'* rejection of ethical and value statements. They believed that value statements were meaningless and adversely affected their ability to be objective in their judgements. Gradually there was an estrangement of science from the humanities. Two quite separate cultures gradually emerged.[3] Subsequently, in post-Enlightenment philosophy, the idea of value-free facts was attacked. However, this was after the separation of science from the humanities had begun.

The reaction of the romantics against science was directed mainly against the physical sciences. An aesthetic sense was retained in the environmental sciences.[4] This may partly explain the jibe against environmentalists as 'antiscientific nature mystics'.[5] More recently the environmental sciences, including the science of ecology, have shifted towards the 'hard sciences'. The respectability of a scientific project is often judged in terms of whether it uses the tools of physics, chemistry and mathematics.

As we noted above the idea that science is value-free was given a philosophical basis in logical positivism. Later, philosophers of science pioneered the idea that there is an imaginative leap of faith in the process

---

[1] E. Hargrove, *Foundations of Environmental Ethics* (Prentice Hall, Englewood Cliffs, 1989) pp.22-26.
[2] R. Attfield, 'Has the History of Philosophy Ruined the Environment?', *Environmental Ethics*, 13,(1991) pp.127-137.
[3] C. P. Snow, *The Two Cultures and the Scientific Revolution* (Cambridge University Press, New York, 1961). Logical positivism is founded on the philosophy of Auguste Comte which recognises only positive facts and observable phenomena and the laws which determine them. All inquiry into causes or ultimate origins is abandoned in this system.
[4] E. Hargrove, *ibid.*, p.77.
[5] J. Passmore, *Man's Responsibility for Nature* (Duckworth, London, 1980).

of scientific discovery.[1] However, the public image of science has not let go completely of the idea that science somehow gives us facts which are value-free. Alongside this faith in science we find a growing distrust in the way science and technology intrudes and is part of our cultural fabric. There is a sense of emptiness which becomes reinforced by the intuition that our highly technologically developed lifestyle is somehow responsible for the destruction of our planet.

(2) The Greening of Theology and Ethics

The collapse of the myth of progress in the wake of historical factors such as the threat of the nuclear holocaust and the ecological crisis led to a crisis of hope in the late 1960's. Jürgen Moltmann urged us to resist the temptation to fall into either a state of presumption in a utopian vision of the future or into a well of despair through loss of hope.[2] What does it mean in terms of the ecological crisis not to succumb to these extremes? The first task of theology is to become aware of the image of God it portrays and the way this shapes our attitudes to each other and the environment. We need to discard images of God which portray him as tyrannical, domineering over creation, and rediscover the Trinitarian relationships which portray God as social, in loving relationship with creation.[3] Moltmann rejects the concept of hierarchical relationships within the Godhead, insisting that the interdependence of God as Trinity is reflected in the interdependence of egalitarian social networks. Moreover, God is present in creation through the cosmic Spirit. The Lutheran, Joseph Sittler, like Moltmann, was one of the first Protestants to recognize the significance of the Orthodox tradition of the cosmic Christ as relevant for an understanding of the meaning of interconnectedness in ecological relationships.[4] In this sense to be faithful to the Christian tradition requires us to be ecological.[5]

We will postpone a full discussion of the way theology informs ethics until the final section. Philosophical ethicists more often than not bracket out theology as we will explain further below. We find different schools of thought emerging in the field of philosophical environmental ethics.[6] These are based on different answers to two basic questions:

(a) Who or what has moral standing, that is what are the criteria for moral consideration?

(b) How do we decide where there is a conflict of interest between entities which both possess the same moral standing?

[1] M. Polanyi, *Personal Knowledge* (Routledge and Kegan Paul, London, 1958).

[2] J. Moltmann, *Theology of Hope* (SCM, London, 1967) pp.22-26.

[3] J. Moltmann, *The Trinity and the Kingdom of God* (SCM, London, 1981) pp. 111-114. For a further discussion of Moltmann's views see C.Deane-Drummond, 'Moltmann's Ecological Theology: A Manifesto for the Greens' in *Theology in Green*, 1 (1992) pp.21-27.

[4] J. Sittler, 'A Theology for Earth' in *The Christian Scholar* 37 (1954) pp.367-374.

[5] V. Rossi, 'Theocentrism: The Cornerstone of Christian Ecology' in *Epiphany*, 6 (1985) pp.8-14.

[6] D. Van de Veer, C. Pierce (eds.), *People, Penguins and Plastic Trees: Basic Issues in Environmental Ethics*. (Wadsworth, Belmont, 1986) p.ix.

Within the first category we find at least seven different criteria used to assess moral standing. These are:

(i) Personhood.

(ii) Potential Personhood. This would, in practice, mean that neo-natal humans have moral standing above that of primates.

(iii) Rationality. This follows from the idea that humans have a greater capacity for reason than other creatures. There can be degrees of rationality in this category.

(iv) Linguistic Capacity. Few will defend this view today as it implies that retarded humans lack moral standing.

(v) Sentience: that is, the ability to feel pleasure or pain. A modification of this view would also include psychological categories of emotion and relationship, as we will discuss further below. Descartes believed that animals lacked sentience and thus moral standing. The American animal liberationist, Paul Singer, is one of the main advocates for extending sentience and moral standing to include animals.[1]

(vi) Being Alive. This draws on Albert Schweitzer's idea of the 'reverence for life'.[2] This is similar to the contemporary view that an attitude of respect for nature is an 'ultimate one'.[3]

(vii) Being an Integral Part of the Ecosystem.

The latter can take the form of panpsychism, that is, all things are alive in some sense, or the earth and atmosphere is a dynamic living system as we find in Lovelock's *Gaia* hypothesis. This revives, after a fashion, the ancient concept of the earth as a Goddess. Weaker forms of this view are that ecological units have moral standing. We will be discussing this topic further in the next section.

The ethical dilemmas involved where there is a conflict of interests becomes more difficult the further we move from (i) to (vii). Various pejorative labels are used by environmental ethicists to express their disdain for certain alternative positions. At the upper end of the scale we find a 'Radical Speciesism' which rejects any constraint in the treatment of animals. At the lower end of the scale we find 'Species Egalitarianism' which treats all species in the same way.[4] The conflict of interests in the

---

[1] P. Singer, *Animal Liberation: A New Ethic for Our Treatment of Animals* (New York Review, New York, 1975).

[2] A. Schweitzer, *Out of My Life and Thought*, C. Campion (ed.) (New American Library, New York, 1953). See also R. F. Nash, *The Rights of Nature: a History of Environmental Ethics*. P. S. Boyer (ed.) (The University of Wisconsin Press, 1989) pp. 55-86.

[3] P. W. Taylor, *Respect for Nature. A Theory of Environmental Ethics* (Princeton University Press, Princetown, 1986) p.190.

[4] See D. Van de Veer, 'Inter Specific Justice' in *People, Penguins and Plastic Trees, op. cit.*, pp.51-56.

latter case becomes resolved simply by giving priority to basic interests over peripheral interests. In theory this should mean that the place on the evolutionary scale is insignificant, so that killing a worm is as irresponsible as murder. Those who adhere to the biocentric view, do not always recognize the practical consequences of their philosophical theory. We will distinguish between biocentrism, which is aligned with (vi), and holism, which is aligned with (vii) in Section 2 below.

It is possible to opt for an approach which recognises the increase in complexity in evolutionary development and gives higher priority to the more psychologically advanced. The exploitation of non-humans is prevented by taking account of their basic interests.[1] The difficulties with this view is that we still have no real way of discerning which interests are peripheral and which ones are basic for a given species. Moreover, how can we detect levels of psychological hierarchy? Once we put psychological factors into the equation we would find unacceptable rejection of those people whose psychological abilities are impaired. Thus this model forms an inadequate basis for discrimination within *Homo sapiens.*

(3)Ethical Terminology

The different criteria used to delineate moral standing have led to considerable confusion in the literature with respect to terminology. In general, we find the debate centred around the meanings of these terms: intrinsic value, inherent value, instrumental value, moral standing and moral significance:

Intrinsic value. This is the positive value of an event or condition in and of itself. Those who use sentience as a criterion relate this to pleasure or pain.[2]

Inherent value. Some ethicists consider that this is a value given to an object by someone else. In the absence of a valuing subject the object has no inherent value. Robin Attfield uses inherent value in a different way to describe creatures which have interests *per se.*

Inherent worth. This concept describes the case where the good of something is realised. Robin Attfield uses *intrinsic value* to express the same idea. It is independent of instrumental value. Tom Regan describes inherent value in these terms. Tom Regan is a well-known animal liberationist and philosopher in environmental ethics.

Instrumental value. This is where the good of something is only in relation to its usefulness to human beings.

[1] The technical name for this view is 'Two Factor Egalitarianism' which introduces a hierarchy based on psychological factors where the interest of the least psychologically advanced organism is subordinated to a like interest of the more advanced organism. Where two beings are the same psychologically and there is a clash between a peripheral interest and a basic interest, the basic interest prevails. Van de Veer's scheme allows for the fact that being a member of *Homo sapiens* does not *per se* automatically justify their preferential treatment compared with animals. (D. Van de Veer, *ibid,* pp.56-57). E. F. Schumacher's discussion of 'levels of being' as we move from the simplest organism to the human person with self-conscious behaviour is also of relevance (see, E. F. Schumacher, *A Guide for the Perplexed,* (Sphere/Abacus, London, 1978) pp.24-35).

[2] P. Taylor, *op.cit.,* pp.73-75.

Robin Attfield shies away from Tom Regan's definition of *intrinsic value* in terms of an organism's own identity and future.[1] Attfield believes that neither consciousness nor sentience nor cognition are necessary for needs and interests, hence both intrinsic and inherent value have to be defined in terms of interests. He points out that the practical consequences of using *sentience* as a criterion is that we could replace trees with plastic ones. It seems to me that Attfield's broader definition in terms of interests is the more satisfactory alternative. Attfield insists that non-human creatures have *inherent value* which gives them *moral standing*.

One view is that 'sentient animals, plants and ecosystems may be of value that counts morally even though they are not themselves moral agents'.[2] Attfield remains less convinced that we can assign *moral worth* to non-humans, that is have their interests realized. He roots his ideas in a model of stewardship which comes from reflection on Old Testament themes.[3] While his interpretation of the idea of stewardship is ecologically sensitive, it may not go far enough in motivating us towards an awareness of interdependence between all living and non-living creation. The model of stewardship still retains the idea of humankind as apart from the world. We need to find ways of giving equal weight to the idea that we are part of nature. Not all philosophers are convinced that the stewardship model has a real basis in Old Testament thought. It is rather too weak a theme to warrant its extensive usage by environmental ethicists.[4] While Attfield is probably accurate in his perception of environmental ethics, his own view seems to demand a theological model that goes beyond that of stewardship. We will take up and expand this theme in Section 4.

---

[1] R. Attfield, *op. cit.*, pp.143-147.
[2] H. Rolston III, *Environmental Ethics: Duties to and Values in the Natural World* (Temple University Press, Philadelphia, 1988) p.39.
[3] R. Attfield, *op. cit.*, pp.34-37. See also J. Hall, *The Steward: A Biblical Symbol Come of Age* (Friendship Press for Commission on Stewardship, New York, 1982).
[4] J. Passmore, *op. cit.*, p.29; P. Gregorios, *The Human Presence: An Orthodox View of Nature*, (WCC, Geneva, 1978) p.88.

2. *GAIA* AND GREEN ETHICS

(1) *Gaia* and Evolution

Darwin's theory of evolution emerged in the culturally optimistic milieu of his time. His views reinforced the sense of progress in the history of the earth with humankind the end product of that history. Humankind believed that it could extend its realm of power over nature. The non-human world of 'nature' could become 'humanized' by the intervention of science and technology. Some scientists believed that evolution was further evidence of the wise Design of a Creator. However, Darwin's theory of evolution removed the requirement for belief in a Creator as it seemed to show that our history could be explained by natural causes. The myth that our future was best secured through Christianity was gradually replaced by faith in scientific progress.[1] The collapse of this ideal has left many floundering in a search for meaning, trapped in a web of technology that now seems beyond human control. The threat of nuclear and ecological disaster has sharpened the spectre that a few out of four billion members of *Homo sapiens*, one species among many thousands, are capable of radically altering the fate of all species and the whole environment.[2]

Lovelock's views challenge:

(a)   The way we conduct science and technology.

(b)   The power of human beings to affect change in relation to the whole planet's persistence.

It is ironical, perhaps, in view of Lovelock's challenge to science, that he arrived at his conclusions after his participation in highly sophisticated space exploration experiments. The earth as seen from space captures the imagination and appears as a 'living being'. The atmosphere around the earth is stable in composition and very different from that of other planets.

The *Gaia* hypothesis claims that we should treat the living organisms and the environment as a single unit which evolve together as a single planetary 'organism'.[3] The theory of evolution claims that species adapt to fit the external environment. Lovelock argues that living beings do not just adapt to external conditions, such as temperature and gaseous composition, but regulate their environment and keep it within certain limits. In the classic theory of evolution the basic hereditary material of each species is distinct. Every individual organism evolves in competition with other members of the same species. In any given environment those individuals which are best suited to external conditions produce the most offspring. Thus the hereditary material of the individuals best *adapted* to their

---

[1] L. Gilkey, *Reaping the Whirlwind. A Christian Intepretation of History* (The Seabury Press, New York 1976), pp.190-195; 319-322.
[2] 'General Introduction' in *People, Penguins and Plastic Trees, op. cit.,* p.2.
[3] J. Lovelock, *The Ages of Gaia* (OUP, Oxford, 1988).

environment persists to the next generation.[1] Lovelock goes beyond current theory of genetics in his supposition that:

(a) The environment is itself controlled by the activities of living organisms.

(b) The earth functions as a whole organism in a way that can be described as planetary 'evolution'.

(c) The direction of evolution is the persistence of life, rather than up the evolutionary scale towards humans.

The scientific arguments which run counter to (a) are that the homeostatic regulation of the environmental conditions could just as easily operate through inorganic feedback processes. Thus regulation need not depend directly on living organisms to act as detectors in the control system.[2] Lovelock uses the model of control systems as that which best describes the way *Gaia* operates. He was accused initially of adopting a view which suggested there was a built-in purpose or *teleology* to *Gaia*. He strongly rejects any suggestion that his hypothesis is teleological in this sense, since he believes that the regulation is a consequence of the way the system works, rather than depending on any forethought. The significance of insisting that life is an integral part of the system has a bearing on the direction of evolution under point (c). The second idea, (b), is also counter to what is generally accepted as genetics. It becomes impossible to imagine or test the complex interaction that would be required to bring about an 'evolution' of the planet. Lovelock is not really justified in using the term 'evolution' in a scientific Darwinian sense. The coupling between cell and organism, organism and species, species and ecosystem, ecosystem and earth becomes progressively looser. Lovelock misrepresents the looseness of this coupling by describing the planet in organismic terminology.

(2) *Gaia* and Human Responsibility

The appeal of *Gaia* is that it claims that life will persist regardless of human conduct. The seeming 'goal-directedness' of *Gaia* towards the persistence of life does not imply that she has freedom of choice in the anthropological sense. While Lovelock insists that *Gaia* is not teleological in the sense of predestination, some sort of consciousness in *Gaia* is

[1] For a summary of historical aspects of the evolution controversy see C. A. Russell, *Cross Currents; Interactions Between Science and Faith*, (Intervarsity Press, Leicester, 1985) pp.141-176.

[2] C. Deane-Drummond, 'God and Gaia: Myth or Reality?', *op. cit.* The details of the arguments that Lovelock has put forward are outside the scope of this short booklet. In brief he has relied on circumstantial evidence which shows that some changes in atmospheric conditions are correlated with algal activity in the oceans. However, this does not prove that the algae 'control' the changes or that such systems operate on a larger global scale. There are also a number of anomalies in the results which do not fit the hypothesis. It is unclear whether the chain of events depends on feedback from living systems, or whether these living systems have a more passive role as part of a dissipative structures. In other words, while living systems are likely to be part of the overall cycle of nutrients, the property of feedback control is not confined to living systems *as such*.

implied by the idea that she reacts in order that life will persist. Darwin's theory encouraged a humanism which burdened us with a weight of responsibility to manage the earth. Once we imagine a mysterious mechanism of planetary evolution which takes care to sustain life regardless of human conduct, the weight of human responsibility seems to be lifted. The logical outcome of this view is that humans will be 'punished' by the planet if they continue to mismanage affairs. We find a return to the fateful and fearful attitude towards nature.[1] The emotive language of punishment implies more than a simple feedback effect characteristic of impersonal control systems. Lovelock is aiming to be scientific while speculating on the possible role for humans. His portrayal of humans as an advanced warning mechanism to alert the whole planet is unsatisfactory.

It seems to me that *Gaia* appeals much more to the religious imagination as that which tries to make sense of the interconnectedness of life. The difference between the holistic and biocentric view is that while the holists argue for moral value to be given to systems, biocentrists give all living creatures including humankind the same moral standing. The biocentric view would encourage every individual creature to be given moral consideration. It is an extension of the 'animal rights' movement. The holistic view, by contrast, draws on the land ethic of Aldo Leopold and more recently Lovelock's *Gaia* hypothesis.[2] An extreme holism argues in favour of ultimate principles of right and wrong derived from a conception of the earth as a supra-organism. The problem with this view is that it seems to weaken the moral worth of individuals.

It is possible to adopt a view that is intermediate between the extremes of 'holism' and 'individualism'. Certain wholes have 'interests' that are morally significant.[3] While wholes can be analysed in terms of their component parts, they do have properties that their elements lack. These are 'unmysterious' properties based on empirical observations. The kind of value attached to such systems depends on the criteria used to assess value that we discussesd in Section 1. Even if we admit to the moral significance of species and ecosystems we have to find ways of resolving the potential clash between individuals and ecosystems. The idea of interconnectedness and relationship may be useful in this context. Individuals share in the value given to such a whole through their interconnectedness with each other in the system. However, where a system, such as *Gaia*, builds in a considerable redundancy, the value given to individuals is diminished. We may need a new terminology to describe the moral value of wholes known as 'systemic value'.[4]

[1] C. Deane-Drummond, 'God and Gaia: Myth or Reality', *op.cit.*
[2] A. Leopold, *A Sand County Almanac* (Oxford University Press, New York, 1949). See also R. Elliot and A. Gare (eds.) *Environmental Philosophy: A Collection of Essays* (Pennsylvannia State Press, University Park, 1983).
[3] L. E. Johnson, A Morally Deep World *(Cambridge University Press, Cambridge, 1991) pp.148ff.*
[4] H. Rolston III, *op. cit.* pp.188ff. Robin Attfield considers that Rolston's definition of systemic value as that which does not depend on the interests of individual parts amounts to giving wholes 'instrinsic value'. R. Attfield, 'Review of H. Rolston III, Environmental Ethics' in *Environmental Ethics,* 11(1989) pp.363-388.

(3) 'Deep' and 'Shallow' Ecology

Those who are concerned to promote the philosophical implications of ecology have coined the terms 'deep' and 'shallow' ecology. The main difference between the two positions is that the former adopts the holistic model as the criterion for moral standing. 'Shallow' ecology, used by 'deep' ecologists in a way which implies a certain superficiality of thought of their opponents, presupposes an ethic of environmental concern in terms of how different policies affect human interests.

We also find a broad divergence between the classic 'environmental ethic' and the new emergent 'ecological ethic'. The latter takes its bearings from an ecological approach in a way which streses the interconnectedness of all species. Those who advocate ecological ethics in a weak form enlarge the value found in humans to include non-humans. More radical versions of ecological ethics give value to ecosystems. Thus a weak form of ecological ethics stresses the interconnectedness of life forms in ecological webs, while a strong form of ecological ethics values the system itself. Lovelock's *Gaia* hypothesis is closer to the more radical end of ecological ethics as it gives value to the whole planetary system of earth. *Gaia* in its philosophical form gives *ultimate* value to earth.

Some philosophers have found Lovelock's ideas 'extraordinarily' suggestive for environmental philosophy.[1] One of its roles has been to shift attention away from anthropocentric concerns. Philosophical ethicists are often nervous about bringing theology into their discussions. They believe that once ethics becomes dominated by theology it is no longer judged by philosophical criteria.[2] We will argue later that a theocentric approach can also shift the concern of environmental ethics away from a form of anthropocentrism that is self-centred. Moreover, a Christian ethic values and welcomes species diversity and individuals in a way that is not possible in a *Gaian* framework. What matters for *Gaia* is the persistence of life, regardless of the number of species eliminated in the process.

When 'deep' ecology draws on Lovelock's ideas it goes beyond his stated intentions which were to develop new ways of tackling science. He is rather naive in his assumption that his occasional comments about the religious significance of *Gaia* will go unnoticed. For example, he claims that he is agnostic in his presuppositions, while at the same time noting that *Gaia* 'is of this Universe and conceivably a part of God. On Earth she is the source of life everlasting, and is alive now, she gave birth to humankind and we are a part of her.'[3]

[1] A. Weston, 'Forms of Gaian Ethics' in *Environmental Ethics*, 9(1987) pp.217-230. See also S. R. Clark, 'Gaia and Forms of Life' in R. Elliot, A. Gare (eds) *Environmental Philosophy: A Collection of Readings* (Open Universitiy Press, Milton Keynes, 1983) pp.183-194; R. Serafin, 'Noosphere, Gaia and the Science of the Biosphere' in *Environmental Ethics*, 10 (1988) pp.121-138.

[2] W. K. Frankena, 'Ethics and the Environment' in K. E. Goodpaster and K. M. Sayre, (eds), *Ethics and the Problems of the 21st Century* (University of Notre Dame Press, Notre Dame, London, 1979) pp.3-20.

[3] J. Lovelock, *Ages of Gaia, op. cit.,* p.204.

The contact with mystical folk religion probably gives *Gaia* its widest appeal. For 'deep' ecologists our selfhood becomes merged in a mystical union with the world in such a way that protection of the world amounts to protection of ourselves.[1] There are convincing arguments which show that many strands in 'deep' ecology are akin to Stoicism.[2] The modern equivalent of the divine Logos is the ecosystem. Matthew Fox and others take *Gaia* as a fact and use it as a normative metaphysical principle. Ecological consciousness and practice become identified with a salvific goal. The Stoics attempted to overcome the alienation felt by the collapse of the city state by painting a picture of the cosmos as 'home'. Now the contemporary vacuum is that left behind by the collapse of a self-congratulatory modernism with its declared anthropocentrism.[3] The ecological consciousness is portrayed in a way which implies it can overcome this felt alienation. The *subtext* remains one of control and domination, rather than encounter, with its risk of failure in transformation.

Tom Regan, similarly, warns against what he terms an 'environmental fascism'.[4] A less extreme version of ecological ethics should encourage us to think and act globally, while resisting any attempt to weaken diversity. For example, what are the principles which need to be applied in the acquisition of natural resources which lie outside national boundaries? Either we advocate individual freedom of explorers to gain from such discoveries, or we opt for shared distribution through international tax. The idea that trees and parks need to have legal rights would have been unheard prior to the cultural shift towards a greater sense of ecological responsibility.[5]

The ecological ethic also seeks to move beyond the traditional debate between preservation and conservation.[6] While the former argues for the protection of all life, regardless of human interests, it fails to deal adequately with those species which are positively harmful to humans. The latter view, on the other hand, values species in terms of their benefit or potential benefit to humanity in areas such as: food source or potential value in medicine; economic benefit; aesthetic value; educational value; genetic diversity and environmental indicators. An ecological stance would include more species in its sphere by recognising the importance of the different members of an ecological network. However, it still does not deal adequately with those species which do not seem to contribute in any significant way to an ecological web.

---

[1] B. Devall and G. Sessions, *Deep Ecology: Living as if Nature Mattered* (Salt Lake City, Utah, 1985), A. Naess, *Ecology, Community and Lifestyle: Ecosophy 1* (Cambridge University Press Cambridge, 1987).

[2] J. Cheney, 'The Neo-Stoicism of Radical Environmentalism' in *Environmental Ethics,* 11 (1989) pp.293-326.

[3] *Ibid,* also R. Ambler, *Global Theology* (SCM, London, 1990) pp.1-8.

[4] For comment see, R.F.Nash, *op. cit.,* pp.159ff.

[5] C. D. Stone, *Earth and Other Ethics; The Case for Moral Pluralism* (New York, 1987).

[6] For a summary see, A. S. Gunn 'Preserving Rare Species' in, T. Regan,(ed) *Earthbound: Introductory Essays in Environmental Ethics* (Waveland Press, Prospect Heights, 1990) pp.289-335.

3. THE CHALLENGE TO AGRICULTURAL TECHNOLOGY

(1) Introduction

Our last section outlined the 'greening' of philosophical environmental ethics to ecological ethics. 'Nature' receives respect in the place of a more instrumental attitude where non-human creation was viewed in terms of human interest or potential interest. This interest in philosophical circles is relatively new and comes after 'a silence of two thousand years'.[1]

Rex Ambler argues that the mode of dominance in the West has shifted from imperial to economic control.[2] There is clash between an expansionist goal characteristic of the will to economic power and ecological limits to such expansion. The 'development' of poor 'underdeveloped' countries in the South came through export of Western technology. There was a quasi-religious hope that application of scientific knowledge would solve the economic problems underlying the misery of poor communities.[3] As a response to this expanionist goal the Two Thirds' world began to demand a redistribution of political, social and economic power. There is still a fear among those working for economic justice that funds will be shunted away from poverty to ecological concerns.[4] However, aid agencies are becoming increasingly aware that a lack of ecological awareness is bound up with the ecological deterioration of land and further poverty. The idea now is that we need to work towards 'development' which is in keeping with the ability of the planet to sustain the growth in human population. A full discussion of the economic and political implications is outside the scope of this Study. We will be confining our attention here to the more specific application of practical ethical questions in agricultural technology. The answers to these questions have had, in practice, an enormous impact on the way humans have related to the natural environment in both the Northern and Southern hemispheres.

Where does this leave science and technology, especially in relation to immediate agricultural practice? Has the split between philosophy and praxis become so deep seated that the scientific and farming communities would not take these issues seriously anyway? The public pressure raised by the animal rights groups has forced agriculture to take up some of these concerns. We will examine in this section some of the practical difficulties in following through a commitment to ecological ethics. The farming community is responding today to the pressure of the seventies which urged more awareness as to the damage wrought by overuse of fertilizers, pesticides etc. Can we expect any additional changes in a group that acts according to economic values and cost-benefit analysis?

[1] R. F. Nash, *op. cit.*, p. 125.
[2] R. Ambler, *op. cit.*, pp. 7ff.
[3] *Ibid*, p.22.
[4] N. J. Faramelli, 'Ecological Responsibility and Economic Justice' in, I. G. Barbour (ed) *Western Man and Environmental Ethics: Attitudes Towards Nature and Technology* (Addison Wesley, Reading, 1973) pp.188-203.

(2) Environmental Critique of Agricultural Practice

Ecological ethics is uncomfortable and considered to be subversive because it demands a radical change in the lifestyle of the West. This goes beyond just a redistribution of power and wealth and involves a change in affluent habits and reversal of exploitation through a reallocation of land rights to poor farmers. Some observers note the irony that 'the political motive behind American food aid and food for peace programmes was to dump surpluses into foreign markets to ensure high farm prices at home'.[1]

The green revolution of the early part of the twentieth century promised food for everyone through use of new high-yielding varieties. The tragedy was that these highly productive monocultures were also more prone to disease and depended on heavy applications of insecticides, fungicides and fertilizers. These chemical applications caused widespread damage to ecological networks and polluted water systems. Rachel Carson's *Silent Spring* was an apt warning to those who were tempted to put too much faith in biotechnology.[2]

So far the environmental critics of modern agriculture point to the dangers of current farm practice in terms of a conservation model rather than a pre-servation model. Examples of such dangers are:

(a) That to public health through fertilizer application, for example nitrates in water used for drinking.

(b) That concerned with resource depletion in:
  (i) Topsoil through intensive farming.
  (ii) Water through massive irrigation schemes which deplete underground reservoirs.
  (iii) Fossil fuels through the mechanization of agriculture.
  (iv) Gene pool through the replacement of natural biodiversity with monocultures.

(c) Ecological disturbance through the impact of pesticides etc.

While the agrochemical industry is not alone in causing ecological damage it has a high profile from environmental critics because it is seen to be more directly concerned with interfering with 'wild' nature. None-theless, a romantic dream of return to wilderness is not necessarily desir-able or feasible. Many critics of modern agricultural practice are urban romantics out of touch with the human need for survival through cultiva-tion of nature. We have been practising agriculture in some form from the beginning of human history. The response by the agrochemical industry to attacks from environmentalists is worth listening to if we are to find realistic and constructive ways to affect change.[3]

(3) The Response of Agrochemistry to Environmental Criticism

(a) The first line of defence against attack from environmentalists is that they are too naive. Farming is a business and so has to aim at efficiency,

---

[1] W. Aiken, 'Ethical Issues in Agriculture' in T. Regan (ed.), *Earthbound op. cit.*, p.261.
[2] R. Carson, *Silent Spring* (Penguin Books, Harmondsworth, 1965).
[3] For a detailed discussion see W. Aiken, *op. cit.*, pp.247-288.

growth and profit. The purpose of agriculture can never be to promote environmental sanctity, ecological stability or resource conservation. Hence the standards by which agriculture should be judged should be those set by business ethics. As long as consumers demand farm products at low prices it is unfair to blame farmers for the damage caused; it is simply a matter of market forces.

This line of defence is worth taking seriously. Can we really hold farmers responsible for their farming practice? The pressure for cheap goods comes from the poorer sections in society. However, the poor and disadvantaged are not in a financial position to buy the more expensive 'environmentally friendly' goods. Market forces are part of Western society which according to the agricultural industry dissolves them of responsibility for causing the damage. Yet the agricultural industry cannot blame society at large for acting irresponsibly. All consumers, not just farmers, have to reexamine their lifestyle.

Ecological ethics does not just challenge agricultural practices, but also questions the economic and political structures of society which forces those caught in the poverty trap to buy cheap goods.[1] It would also be naive to assume that a change in politics would automatically solve economic problems. The ecological crisis is even more severe in totalitarian regimes.[2] Nonetheless, every democratic society should give its citizens the freedom to adopt an ecologically friendly lifestyle. This freedom might only be possible if each citizen has an income above a certain minimum basic level.

(b) The second line of defence by the agrochemical industry is that abuses are exaggerated. They compare themselves favourably with other major polluting industries such as coal or chemical refineries. However, in terms of ethics, this is a very weak line of defence. Environmental problems are very real and have a cumulative effect and all those responsible share the blame.

(c) A third line of defence is that science itself will solve the ecological problems, such as discovering new ways to provide energy resources. However, this argument does not take the ecological limits to growth seriously enough. If we rely on market forces alone to address the problem the ecological abuse will have reached such a pitch that we will be near collapse. It is nave to expect cosmetic inventions in biotechnology to achieve more than a delay in the onset of the crisis.

(d) One final line of defence which we raised briefly above is that environmentalists have their priorities confused. The practice of intensive agriculture for humanitarian reasons must inevitably involve the sacrifice of

[1] This problem might be eased if there was an adoption of a scheme known as Basic Income. This scheme proposed that all citizens have a right to a basic income regardless of age, sex or colour and whether in paid employment or not. See T. Walter, *Basic Income* (Marion Boyars, London, 1988); S. Brittan and S. Webb, *Beyond the Welfare State: An Examination of Basic Incomes in a Market Economy* (Aberdeen University Press, 1990).
[2] For comment on this see J. Moltmann, *Creating a Just Future* (SCM, London, 1989) pp.51-55.

environmental quality. But is there really a choice between stressing the environment or ignoring the poor? The protection of the environment can go alongside changes in lifestyle habits of the affluent and the redistribution of land rights. In other words if consumption in the West was reduced by a small fraction this would provide the resources for the redistribution of land in the two thirds world. The ecological burden of the population explosion is also related to this issue. It is not enough just to consider numbers of peoples, but consumption of resources per capita.[1]. It would be unwise to suggest that the resolution of these problems is simple or straightforward. The complexity and political instability of many poorer countries hampers the attempts to arrive at a global consensus in terms of environmental protection. Furthermore, those most powerless to respond to environmental damage, such as that caused by the greenhouse effect, are often the least responsible for creating the damage.[2]

(4) The Case For Animal Rights
What kind of changes can we expect if the voices of more radical environmentalists become popular? Tom Regan believes that the initial period of ridicule has given way to discussion and the time is now ripe for implementation.[3] The more radical animal rights groups campaign for:

(a) The abolition of the use of animals in science.

(b) The dissolution of commercial agriculture.

(c) The elimination of commercial and sport hunting and trapping.

The animal rights groups challenge the assumption that non-human creation is a resource to be used for human benefit. We need to discriminate between the factory farming of animals and the use of animals in poorer countries where human survival is at stake.

The philosophy of holism is that of the biotic community of equals.[4] It is rather doubtful if any form of agriculture would be possible if this model was adopted since even organic farming is disruptive of soils and natural habitats. We would have to take up the simple lifestyle of hunter/gatherers of our early ancestors.[5] A more realistic goal would be one which aims to be compatible with ecosystems and minimizes violence and disruption of the environment.

(5) Ecohumanism
The option of ecohumanism distances itself from both holism and anthropocentrism. It is concerned for people and individuals alongside living in a way which is compatible with the wider ecological home. The only

[1] R. Ambler, op. cit., pp.48-51. For obligations to future generations see R. Attfield, op. cit., pp.88-114.
[2] D. H. Gleick, 'Climate Change and International Politics: Problems Facing Developing Countries' in Ambio, 18(1989) pp.333-339.
[3] T. Regan, 'The Case for Animal Rights' in D. Van de Veer and C. Pierce, (eds), People, Penguins and Plastic Trees, op. cit., pp.32-39.
[4] J. B. Callicott, 'Elements of an Environmental Ethic: Moral Considerability and the Biotic Community', Environmental Ethics, 1 (1979) pp.71-81.
[5] W. Aiken, op. cit., pp.269-270.

ecologically damaging behaviour that is justified is where the basic survival needs of humans were at stake. Ecological efficiency is not the same as economic efficiency. The former is the conscientious adoption of agricultural practices to suit local conditions.[1]

An example of using the earth's resources in an ecologically efficient way is a possible shift in crop management. Instead of producing luxury goods we could grow necessary foods and fibres. Ecological efficiency would also take into account regenerative practices and complementary technology using local skills. There are both long term and short term goals in ecologically efficient management of land. In the short term use of fertilizers and pesticides could be cut back or removed, while in the long term different crops could be introduced.

An ecological ethic requires us to be more rounded in our educational methods so that the importance of human responsibility becomes part of the education of scientists and agriculturalists. While ethicists have become involved in the policy decision making in areas such as genetic engineering, the time may be ripe for a much greater recognition of the importance of ethical considerations across broader subject areas. Some of the roots of the environmental crisis will be dealt with by raising the consciousness of the impact of the shape and direction of agricultural biotechnology.

[1] *Ibid.*, pp.277ff.

4. A CHRISTIAN CRITIQUE

(1) Introduction

One of the dilemmas of the theological method is what we take as our starting point. Is it the critical and social issues of our contemporary culture? Or do we begin with knowledge of God and let religious beliefs frame the questions and the answers? So far we have presupposed a core belief in God as Creator who exists in Trinitarian relationships. Sytematic theology is struggling to come to an understanding of God that takes into account the full implications of the ecological crisis.[1] It is our intention here to develop a way of engaging in a dialogue between systematic theology and philsophical ethics in order to offer some orientation in an area of inquiry which has begun to 'go wild'.[2]

If we find absolute moral value in ecological systems we are letting ecology take the place that was traditionally occupied by theology.[3] Once we give nature absolute moral value or goodness it becomes difficult to distinguish between conflicting interests. It is possible that a more appropriate way to express the harmony in ecological relationships is through poetic and aesthetic categories of beauty rather than moral categories of goodness. There is, however, also a discernable link between poetry and ethics. Ascribing value effectively can arise from non ego-centric viewing which is encouraged by a poetic freedom from self. In this way humans become compassionate enough to value all things. We will address the question as to whether aesthetic values are sufficient to develop an ecological ethic.

One of the attractions of the *Gaia* hypothesis to philosophical ethicists is the idea of *Sophia* archetype. *Sophia* brings us salvation through the resacralization of nature. Those who take ecology as the basis for their philosophy describe their approach as *Ecosophy* 1 where *sophy* is derived from the Greek word for wisdom, or *sophia*.[4] Once *Ecosophy* becomes a normative system it sets up a division between those with and without 'ecological consciousness'. While Matthew Fox claims that the basis for his cosmology is ecology, he also invites us to 'trust one's inner voice'.[5] We are now moving beyond rational argument and debate in a way which excludes those who do not share this experience. Once we construct

---

[1] It is only possible to give an outline sketch here of the greening of systematic theology. For a summary of theological models see K. Innes, *op. cit.,* 17-22. For biblical theology's contribution to the debate see J. Rogerson, *Genesis 1-11, Old Testament Guides* (JSOT Press, Sheffield, 1991). For a detailed academic discussion see, R. Murray, *The Cosmic Covenant* (Sheed and Ward, London,1992).

[2] Holmes Rolston III puts value in nature as wilderness hence the title of his book, *Philosophy Gone Wild* (Prometheus Book, Buffalo, 1989). Peter Wenz argues that Holmes Rolston's philosophy mixes poetry, prose and scientific information in a way which makes it disorganized in his argument. P. S. Wenz 'Review of H. Rolston III' in *Environmental Ethics,* 100 (1989) pp. 195-197.

[3] A. Carson 'Review of Philosophy Gone Wild, R. Rolston III', *Environmental Ethics* 8 (1986) pp.163-177.

[4] D. Davies, 'Ecosophy, The Seduction of Sophia', *Environmental Ethics* 8 (1986) pp.151-162

[5] J. Cheney, *op. cit.,* pp.310ff. See M. Fox, *Original Blessing,* (Bear, Santa Fe, 1986)

ecological consciousness as a means for overcoming alienation it can become a totalizing and colonizing attitude. The ethical mandate becomes grounded in the 'authoritarian impersonal truth of metaphysics'.[1] An alternative, more authentic, approach is to accept diversity in a way which is not condescending towards those who are 'anthropocentric'.

(2) The Place of Humans

Our task here is not so much to dismiss the idea of stewardship, which draws on the anthropocentic models, but to show how there are additional ways of creating models from the Christian tradition. Anthropocentrism that is self-centred can lead to an unacceptable faith in the power of human potential. Ecological consciousness on its own can lead to an unacceptable faith in the planet, *Gaia*. Both the anthropocentric and ecological paradigms can be reinterpreted in terms of a theocentric ethic. So far there has been a predominance of theocentric ethics, especially in Protestant theology, which presupposed models of stewardship as the only way of relating humankind and creation. Once we come to understand God in categories of loving relationship rather than categories of authority and sovereignty, it allows for an understanding of ethics that is other-centred kept within the boundaries of Christian faith. It seems to me that while the stewardship model can be reinterpreted in such a way that it encourages a responsible attitude towards creation and stresses the special dignity of humans, it may not go far enough to meet the challenge of the ecological crisis.

The Orthodox tradition of the East offers a way of setting human life in a cosmic and natural context that encourages us to view human life as made for the cosmos rather than *vice versa*. Historically Western Christian ethics has assumed that good for human beings coincided with the ultimate divine purpose. The biblical tradition puts emphasis on the action of God in human history. However, those elements in the tradition which enlarge the scope of God's action to include the whole cosmos have been neglected in the history of interpretation of these texts in the West. We might ask ourselves whether the power of the Creator inevitably orientates itself towards the well being of humankind.[2] The cosmic elements to the Noahic covenant between the whole creation and God would suggest otherwise.[3] The cosmic Christ as portrayed in Colossians 1 would also suggest that God's purpose is directed towards the well being of the whole creation, not simply towards human concerns. The idea of restraint in human action need not imply that the special dignity of human beings is lost. The temptation to allow 'nature' to become romanticized in a biocentric ethics could lead to violent action towards humans who are behaving in a way which continues to treat 'nature' as a resource. There is a difference between respect for nature as part of God's creation, and reverence for nature which can border on pantheism.

Our knowledge of the mutual interdependence of all creation should encourage a mutual humility and respect between persons and between

[1] J. Cheney, *op. cit.*, p.311.
[2] J. M. Gustafson, *op. cit.*, pp.81ff.
[3] R. Murray, *op. cit.*,

persons and the non-human creation. While we cannot justify arrogant claims about the future purpose of God for creation, we can insist on an image of God which stresses his loving relationship with creation. The Christian belief in the Incarnation inevitably points to the special dignity of humans, yet it also assures us that all of nature can become a sacrament which expresses the love of God.

There is a difference between finding solidarity in and with the creation in a way which welcomes our interdependence and finding in nature a basis for moral significance. Once we adopt the latter we become confronted with the theodicy question, recast in terms of the problem of evil in the natural world. The harsh reality of biological existence is that one creature's evil is another's good. Holmes Rolston seems to assume that evolution will press towards an Ultimate Good. In a subtle way he has introduced the myth of progress under the guise of a form of 'Naturalism'.[1] But this is a fallacy long exposed by ethicists: ethics is not so much a mirror held up to nature as a light which is created by communities for their own purposes in dialogue with their environment.

(3) The Future of Creation

One of Moltmann's significant achievements has been to point us away from the myth of the cycles of nature and the return to the early paradisaical state to a new future heralded by the death and resurrection of Christ.[2] This contrasts sharply with the view of Rolston discussed above where he understands the resurrection in continuity with the cycles of nature. Now Christianity's symbol of Easter 'did not so much replace as complement, enrich and extend the primitive and universal impulse in us to celebrate the warmth of spring and resurgence of life that is given by the mysterious powers of the sun'.[3] Moltmann puts greater emphasis on the forward movement of human history and he integrates nature and history without loss in proper respect for creation.[4] One difficulty with Moltmann's position is that he tends to concentrate too much on the transformation of creation and corporate celebration in the future without giving enough consideration to present biological reality.

The Orthodox and Catholic tradition of nature as sacrament is rooted in gospel accounts of Jesus' use of natural elements such as water, bread and wine to express spiritual truths. The biblical affirmation of natural world is also part of the Pauline tradition such as Romans 1. The Old Testament theme of a covenant between God and all creatures encourages us

---

[1] A. Carson *op. cit.*, Carson accuses Rolston of being naturalist. However, Rolston is not naturalist in the classical philosophical sense as he would then completely ignore the existence of spiritual laws and base his morality on natural laws alone. He seems to welcome spirituality, but it is still difficult to decipher the basis on which this spirituality rests. For example, Rolston is anxious for us to 'take the experiential plunge into nature, mixing participatory immediacy and reflective distance, reason and emotion, romance and criticism, nature and spirit ... We go out into the field. We go wild', p.221.
[2] J. Moltmann, *God in Creation* (SCM, London,1985), p.104ff.
[3] H. Rolston, *Philosophy Gone Wild, op. cit.,* p.259.
[4] Ibid, pp.124-137, J. Moltmann, *The Way of Jesus Christ* (SCM, London, 1990) pp.277ff.

to welcome the fellowship of praise given to God by all creation.[1] By involving ourselves in this celebration we are not looking to the planet to provide the continuity of life, as in *Gaia*, or to ecological unity itself as a fantasy inherited from earlier cosmology, but to a common Creator who invites all creation into fellowship. Once we come to appreciate fully this sacramental aspect of creation our strength of resolve against all abuse of creation is sharpened. It is not so much a return to the static cosmology of earlier centuries before the Enlightenment, but an awareness of the participation of all creation in the love of the Creator. This appreciation of the dynamic movement between God and creation is also helped by the visual and verbal arts which lead us away from self-centredness. The stewardship model may convince us in a rational sense that we need to act responsibly towards creation. However, the liturgical, sacramental model of fellowship involves us more as whole persons.

(4) Towards a Theocentric Approach

How does the above sacramental view of creation affect hard ethical choices such as which species should survive where it is in our power to make such choices? We need gifts of wisdom and discernment in making such choices as well as rational insight. A theocentric ethic of ecological responsibility would press for the maintenance of species diversity, whether they are closest to human interest or part of the ecological web. A Christian critique would reisist making such decisions based on economic resources and cash value of species. The extreme biocentric view is that human life is an evil where it is preserved at the expense of non-human creation. A Christian critique would insist that this approach does not give sufficient dignity to human life. In other words while a theocentric ethics would value all of creation, there is a measure of hierarchy built into the discernment of choices between survival of species. A thoroughgoing egalitarian approach makes practical choices between species impossible. However, the measure of hierarchy between species need not apply within the human community. The idea that all species be preserved at whatever cost has to be compromised in some circumstances.

We suggested earlier that aesthetic categories might help us define the value of 'nature'. This is more than just attractiveness to individuals, but an awareness that anything that is needs to be permitted to exist. Hargrove's idea that an aesthetic category has an ontological sense moves us beyond the idea that the value given is a matter of personal opinion.[2] The difficulty with Hargrove's ontological interpretation is that it seems to suggest that anything other than wilderness that is untouched by human contact is less than the best. There are few ecologies in Europe that are not in some sense affected by humankind. An ontological argument for environmental ethics seems to leave human beings powerless to affect any responsible

[1] R. D. Sorrell, *St.Francis of Assisi and Nature: Tradition and Innovation in Western Christian Attitudes toward the Environment*, (Oxford University Press, Oxford, 1988). Moltmann uses the idea of friendship with nature, but this is based on Christ's friendship with us and seems to point to the new creation. For further comment see, C. Deane-Drummond, 'A Critique of Jürgen Moltmann's Green Theology', in *New Blackfriars, November*, (1992) pp.554-565.

[2] E. C.Hargrove, *op. cit.*, pp. 165-195.

choices. According to this view the history of 'nature' becomes restricted and limited by human intervention.[1] A form of ecohumanism discussed in the last section seems to fit in most easily with a theocentric ethic. This both avoids an overly romantic view of nature, but allows our shared celebration of its beauty before God to shift us away from a purely selfish form of humanism.

It is obvious that there are no easy or readily defined answers. The complexity of human involvement with nature becomes more acute once we reflect on the religious pluralism as a context for theocentric ethics. The difficulty in dialogue between different faiths may be one of the reasons why moral philosophers have preferred to bracket off questions about God altogether. However, an ecological consciousness within a Christian framework should encourage us to engage in dialogue with other members of the human family. There may be areas of common concern which will allow us to reach agreement in terms of ethical practice. Kung's suggestion that a new world ethic will emerge from a sense of global responsibility seems to be rather over optimistic.[2] The particular and unique contribution of each faith has to be allowed to develop. The unity comes from the recognition and affirmation of diversity and mutual respect between faiths, rather than a non-differentiated mystical union which ignores difference. Christian uniqueness does not imply lack of dialogue, but a realism about the possible emptiness of a common unified religion where all distinctions become lost.[3]

The purpose of this study is to show how the move towards ecological thinking challenges our perception of theology and ethics. We can allow a theocentric ethic to emerge which welcomes the interconnectedness in creation while not losing sight of the special dignity of humans and all individual creatures. The Christian faith in God as Creator is relevant to the way we ascribe value to ourselves in the context of the whole cosmos. Our faith in God as Creator and Redeemer should encourage us in our hope that real changes are possible and practicable. Our faith in God as loving all his creatures should enable us to imitate that love in working to curb the excesses of greed and exploitation of creation which have surfaced throughout human history. Our Christian tradition can still speak with relevance in helping us to forge a path through the labyrinth of debates over philosophical ethics and ecological praxis.

---

[1] *Ibid*, p.195.
[2] H. Kung. *Global Responsibility* (SCM, London, 1990) For a review see, C. Deane-Drummond, *Theology in Green,* 3 (1992) pp.41-43.
[3] G. D'Costa, (ed), *Christian Uniqueness Reconsidered* (Orbis, New York, 1990).

POSTSCRIPT—A PRAYER

O God: grant us a deeper sense of fellowship
with all living things,
Our little brothers and sisters,
to whom in common with us
You have given this earth as home.

We recall with regret that in the past
We have acted high handedly and cruelly
in exercising our domain over them.
Thus, the voice of the earth
which should have risen to you in song
has turned into a groan of travail.

May we realize that all these creatures also live
for themselves and for you
not for us alone.
They too have the goodness of life,
as we do,
and serve you better in their way
than we do in ours.

*Prayer for a Deeper Sense of Fellowship with
All Living Things. St Basil of Caesarea (329-379)*